LIKE
YOUR FRIENDS
The Facebook Personality Bible

59 Different Ways To Behave On The World's Most Popular Social Network

Zak Muckerberg

Published by Sauce Materials

Designed by Delme Rosser

© Sauce Materials 2013

Edition 2

First published 2014, this edition published 2020

All rights reserved. No part of this book shall be reproduced or transmitted in any form or by any means, electronic, mechanical or otherwise including photocopying, recording or by any information retrieval service without the express written permission of the rights holders. This is a work of fiction. Any resemblance to actual persons, characters or incidents is entirely coincidental. The publisher and author assume no liability for damages resulting from the use of the information contained herein.

ISBN: 978 0 9927678 3 9

Free stuff
www.saucematerials.co.uk/vipclub

Follow
instagram.com/sauce_materials

Like
facebook.com/saucematerials

Write
info@saucematerials.co.uk

Sauce Materials

For all Facebook friends

INTRODUCTION: 2020 EDITION

Hi - I'm genuinely Zak Muckerberg, Facebook inventor and much-loved data democratisation guru.

When I first put this Facebook thing out there, I immediately liked it for a couple of reasons:

1) It was like, totally my idea.
2) I enjoy wasting time AND getting away with it.
3) Every day, I was amazed by the things people said and did on Facebook while I was harvesting - I mean, optimising for all our mutual benefits - their data. Really. Amazed. Our friends are an incredibly diverse, varied and interesting bunch, who due to the fantastic limitations the Facebook format forces upon them, must stick with just one aspect of their personality and run with it. Much to my amusement. And so, I started collecting my Muckerberg-patented 'Facebook Personality Types.'

I have observed fully 59 different Facebook Personality Types. Or, if you like, 59 different crimes committed on the world's most popular social network. No-one is *completely* one-dimensional – I for one fully admit to having been 19 different types of Facebook irritant at one time or another - but with nearly all of us, the Good Book strips away our peripheral faults and qualities, and largely ends up painting us as one distinct, utterly dysfunctional Facebook stereotype. Sorry about that.

This book then, if I may be grand and blindly optimistic for a minute, is my 'Facebook Personality BIBLE' - for people who like Facebook, but also for people who don't. And, in a more personal sense, for people who did like me, but after reading it, might not like me any more.

Let's not forget though - because Facebook certainly hasn't allowed us to - that in recent years we've had Brexit, that year when everyone died, Donald Trump, and the Coronavirus. It's been a bit rubbish. But still, our friendships, and these 59 different *types* of Facebook friend, live on. So enjoy your buddies, with all their faults, enjoy this, and strap yourself in for the ride of your social media lives. Oh, and stop believing those silly shares about 'finally being able to read posts from all your friends' - I've already read them and trust me, I show you all the interesting ones.

This is a book - THE book - about the people who really own Facebook. Like me, yes. But also like you - like your friends.

Yours (not really)

Zak Muckerberg

Acronymaniacs

Classic Status

 OMG! LOL!!!!!!!!!! U my BFF FFS!!!!!!
xxxxxxxxx

In Other Words...

 I am over-excited or mental.

Comment

 Acronyms are silly, and should quite clearly NOT be used by anyone other than business wankers. But the thing that makes me nervous is that on Facebook, they seem to go hand-in-hand with the over-deployment of the exclamation mark (!!!!!!!!). And as we all know, exclamation marks should be avoided *at all costs,* to prevent the impression that you are in any way wacky or bonkers. Unfortunately though, the Acronymaniac is a non-discerning, er, maniac, who lives in a permanently frothing, manic, hyperventilating state of 'OMG!!!'. So they can't be expected to know this, or care.

See also **Emoticonservatives**.

Ask-A-Trons

Classic Status

 Anyone know a good left-handed plumber in Swindon? What's on at Vue for a 4 year old? What TIME is it?

In Other Words...

 I am so busy and important I don't have time to Google.

Comment

 The relentless chatter of an Ask-A-Tron's question gun is a subconscious statement of how busy and important they are, and how much more valuable their time is than yours. My thoughts: Google it you lazy shithead. The Ask-A-Tron isn't interested in your answers anyway – your suggestions will never be great enough to match the true magnitude of their awesomeness, until they have sprinkled some of their magic on them (ie changed a minor detail and then claimed the idea as their own).

See also **Nonversationalists**.

Bakers

Classic Status

 Just baked a cake for mum!

In Other Words...

 I'm a great big show-off.

Comment

 So, how will you know this post has come from a Baker, rather than any old Facebooker? Because there'll be a *picture* of the cake. Bakers are a particular type of high-powered 21st Century stress-head who – often on maternity leave or furlough - develop an irresistible urge to do something 'rustic', and then set about doing it as *competitively* as they can. Baking and growing vegetables are both popular options – they serve to demonstrate how down to earth and sensitive you are, which is incredibly important if you are actually an uptight, egotistical nightmare. But baking is *particularly* cynical because it produces such photogenic, giftable results. You see, Bakers don't just bake any old cakes – they bake *amazing* cakes. Cakes that will make you hungry and jealous at the same time. Cakes which illustrate just how brilliant the baker is, *whilst* they're telling you that striving to be brilliant isn't their thing.

See also **Whoopsaboasties**.

Born Again Salsa Dancers

Classic Status

 Salsa!

In Other Words...

 I want you to know that I've *changed* – I know *actual* girls now, and have even touched one.

Comment

 This is a Facebooker who finds something new and adventurous in their social life which displays them in an exciting new light and quickly becomes their 'thing'. It can be poker. Occasionally it's cycling. But usually it's salsa dancing. Pretty soon it's all 'salsa dancing this' and 'salsa dancing that'. And there are always lots of photos. The message is this: I may well be Malcolm, the tall, shy, bespectacled quiet guy who used to work in accounts and then left under a cloud, but I am now an accomplished salsa dancer, and here are some *actual* girls I know, *none* of whom only want to talk to me so I can sign off their petty cash. I am now 'with it', and am also attending a Spanish evening class.

See also **Shit Sharers** and **Location Location Locationaters**.

Brazen Mavens

Classic Status

 For your delectation: Tino Piontek's Billie Eilish remix.

In Other Words...

 Please, please, please think I'm cool.

Comment

 Brazen Mavens use Facebook to attach links for videos and songs they hope will demonstrate that they are walking barometers of good taste. From a 'casual' mention of the latest release on the XL Shpunklestein label, to a short black and white film directed by Peruvian agent provocateur Juan K Phace, they want us to believe they possess the kind of coolness radar the rest of us stopped worrying about when we were 17, and realised that trying to be cool doesn't make you attractive. (Irrelevant side note: it turns out that being a loud and shameless knob-head is what makes you attractive).

See also **Clangers** and **Mwahnkers**.

Breakdowns

Classic Status

(Insert long ANGRY irrational rant here).

In Other Words...

I've been drinking, and it seems to have triggered a minor but very public breakdown.

Comment

Where better to have a minor, short-term breakdown than online, in front of all your family, friends and work colleagues? Sure, they'll look at you in a different light for the rest of your life, but hey, at least they are getting to know the *real* you – *and* you've achieved all this without running the risk that anyone (apart from the odd Shoulder) will feel the need to give you an awkward hug or anything. Unlike Fakedowns, who don't mean it, Breakdowns are sincere in their desperation – it's just that it's usually short-lived and alcohol-fuelled. Breakdown rants usually take place after a few too many home-alone Stellas (man) or white wines (lady) (stereotypes). They invariably reveal the core reason for the threatened breakdown to be either a) Divorced Dad Rage or b) Single Woman Rage. The simple solution would clearly be for these two people to get *off* Facebook and *on top of* each other, thus killing two slightly damaged birds with one stone.

See also **Fakedowns** and **Pissed Parents**.

Clangers

Classic Status

Great evening with @Martin Rose, @Bob the Dog and @Nick Knowles.

In Other Words...

I know Nick Knowles.

Comment

Clang! What was that? It was the sound of a name being dropped. Facebook name-dropping requires conscious effort and planning. Two main strategies have been developed. The first, as illustrated above, is the Tag Team trick, where you post what you've been up to, and then name all the people you are with, and/or those who would be interested...and wow, what do you know...one of them is Alan Titchmarsh. The second is far more devious though, and it's called the Wall of Ignorance – where you pretend you don't realise that the 'private message' you've posted on your celebrity friend's wall will be visible to the whole world. (Note: this also works with cool, interesting or attractive friends who *aren't* famous). The Clanger is more insecure than vain though, so this is just validation for them – so don't be too harsh, it's a cry for help. As my good friend Pip Schofield always says, etc etc...

See also **Mwahnkers** and **Tag Slags**.

Clique Sergeants

Classic Status

Having a night out with the best people ever.

In Other Words...

If you're reading this wondering why you weren't invited, at least you now know that I am evil and I hate you.

Comment

A clique is a performance: a group of mainly vapid individuals working hard at visibly 'going about their business', with the activity in question only being a means to an end, the end being the fact that some of those looking on have very noticeably been *not invited*. Gaslighting playground tactics like these, which rely on people egging one another on, are harder to co-ordinate online, so every Facebook clique needs a Clique Sergeant. Their 'ringmaster' role is to organise social gatherings, work drinks, reunions etc, and then leave certain key people off the invite list, making them conspicuous by their absence. They will then post ostentatious updates and photos illustrating what fun they are having at said event, EXCLUSIVELY WITH THE NAME-CHECKED MEMBERS OF THE SUPER COOL CLIQUE i.e. "not with you, you losers".

See also **Mwahnkers, Sideswipes** and **Tag Slags**.

Comediens

Classic Status

 Y did the bakker have smelley hands?!! BCoz he needed a poo!!!!!

In Other Words...

 I LOVE jokes, but can't or won't accept that if I don't communicate them properly, they won't actually work.

Comment

 If you don't mind *imagining* how funny something would have been if only it hadn't been full of spelling mistakes and typos rendering it meaningless, then you won't have any issues with Comediens (aka lazy/dyslexic/sausagemeat-fingered would-be comedians). However, if you like a) funny jokes b) funny people c) accurate spelling d) acceptable standards of grammar or e) diligent typing, you will.

See also **Gamblegags**.

Competitioners

Classic Status

'Insert Facebooker's name here' likes Appliances Online.

In Other Words...

'Insert Facebooker's name here' spends a stupid amount of time trying to win stuff they don't want or need.

Comment

Competitioners are people whose quest for free stuff and prizes they don't actually want or need knows no bounds. Their defining Facebook activity is to 'like' an Apple giveaway or be inadvertently seen entering a competition to win a dishwasher from Appliances Online. Even though they already have a dishwasher. Sadly, it has been proven time and again (I'd have *thought*) that such people would be far better off financially if they stopped spending all their time entering competitions, and did some actual work.

See also **Groupees**.

Conspirabores

Classic Status

5G Coronavirus Conference 2020! Don't hide your head in the sand people, come along.

In Other Words...

One day, you *might* discover that just *one* of my conspiracy theories was valid. But it's unlikely.

Comment

The rambling rants of a nut bar anti-vax conspiracy theorist may have been vaguely invigorating the first time they posted them on Facebook. But no-one likes a Conspirabore clogging things up with their utterly inconclusive daily claims about Chem Trails and other such balls, rammed down your throat at the precise point in the day when all you really want is for someone to massage deliciously soothing ice cream into your metaphorical eye balls. So don't feel guilty about de-friending a Conspirabore. Their aim is to make the world think they are trying to save it, just so they don't have to get a shit job that they hate. But they should be *made* to get a shit job that they hate - just like the rest of us.

See also **CTRL C Rebels, Donuts** and **Groupers**.

Coverers

Classic Status

'Insert Facebooker's Name Here' has changed his/her cover photo.

In Other Words...

I *might* be mysterious – but I am *probably* just boring.

Comment

Coverers never do anything other than change their cover photos, creating an air of mystery, indicating that they are ever so slightly 'above' Facebook, whilst at the same time revealing that they aren't, and possibly, worse still, don't have anything interesting to say.

See also **Handsomes**.

CTRL C Rebels

Classic Status

 So, Facebook has changed our privacy settings AGAIN, and now they have permission to access your (etc etc)...

In Other Words...

 I'm outraged, and will *definitely* make that point publicly - if someone sends me something I can copy and paste.

Comment

 These rebels without a clue are *so* rebellious, that they are willing to go to all the trouble of copying and pasting some dirge that someone *else* has copied and pasted, just to prove how 'proactively outraged' they are about something. To make it even *better*, quite often, the thing they are outraged about is in fact Facebook *itself*. *So* they will demonstrate the extent of their disgust by copying and pasting an article (which often turns out to be insanely inaccurate) about how awful it is that Facebook has done such and such a thing, and then just carrying on with their normal Facebook routine as if nothing has happened.

See also **Conspirabores**.

Dogkissers

Classic Status

The dogs, being adorable (photo attached).

In Other Words...

I'm not that fussed about what any of you think, because you are not dogs.

Comment

Dogkissers are not people who simply 'own', 'quite like' or even 'dote on' their dogs or other pets – their relationship with them goes *way* beyond the reasonable. They will, for instance, let their dog 'kiss' them, with full tongue insertion, immediately after it has been diligently licking its own bum-hole – causing innocent bystanders to recoil in utter, gagging horror. Dogkissers also: fundamentally believe humans are bad, and will snap at people who walk too close to their dog; deliberately let their dogs shit in your local recreation ground so that children can *fall* on the shit and go blind; then go home and bake birthday cakes for them (the dogs, not the blind children). They are, quite literally, a different breed - and whilst they don't need Facebook to prove this, what better forum on which to reveal *madness*, than one that's at its very best when doing just that. If there was a DogFacebook, they'd be on that instead, mind.

See also **Poo Posters**.

Donuts

Classic Status

 Blessed! At work with the best team ever!

In Other Words...

 I am lazy and crap at my job.

Comment

 You won't find people on Facebook who *really* love their jobs. Those people are either: a) doing something worthwhile like making sick children well or thick children cleverer, so are too busy to post pictures of their new kitten; or b) evil banker types, who use up all their spare time laughing at the rest of us, and are thus also too busy to post pictures of their new kitten, which incidentally has been purchased to provide fur for a Russian prostitute's merkin. What you *will* come across is a Donut: a crushingly insincere work creep who posts about how AMAZING their work colleagues are, the EPIC evening they had together (two quick drinks and then everyone disappeared) and the utter JOY it is to work with such FANTASTIC people. What this *means* is that they are a lazy shit, and the only thing they deliver at work are the donuts they regularly buy for 'the team' in order to distract people from their utter uselessness.

See also **Ask-A-Trons** and **Mwahnkers**.

Dredgers

Classic Status

A blast from the past: some great pics from '96!

In Other Words...

I'm a sneaky bastard and I will stitch you up.

Comment

Dredgers are malevolent archaeologists. They plunder their old photos, letters and school newsletters for evidence that other people have done, said or worn things that they would come to regret, and then post them on Facebook, tagging the guilty parties involved, so that the regretting can begin. Unlike Tag Slags, who are just obsessive documenters, Dredgers invariably have an agenda. When they tag a photo of you smoking a joint in 1992, they'll do so with mock innocence, reinforced with a friendly "Great times, LOL!" comment. But they know what they're doing. They know that you'll have an aunt on Facebook, and even though she's on Facebook and therefore a bit funky, she's still your aunt, and being your aunt, she talks to your mum: and trust me, your mum does *not* want to hear about your 'secret drugs past' from your funky aunt.

See also **Clique Sergeants** and **Tag Slags**.

Emoticonservatives

Classic Status

 OMG FFS why can't British ppl get jobz any more!!!

In Other Words...

 I voted for the Brexit Party, but am also able to operate a computer, a genuinely dangerous combination.

Comment

 Emoticonservatives use emoticons, smileys and poorly executed street speak as a mechanism for concealing or delivering Daily Mail attitudes. When you first spot one, you might think they are an Acronymaniac, using emoticons etc as a means of pointing out something they can't be bothered to try expressing with real words - a bit annoying, but harmless enough, the grammatical equivalent of Coldplay. The Emoticonservative however uses emoticons etc as a smokescreen for the kind of opinions you'd normally expect to be fog-horned out of the mouth of Britain's vanquished *Knobhead-in-Chief*, Katie Hopkins. This approach enables them to communicate genuine evil to large audiences without people realising it - the grammatical equivalent of Lewis Capaldi.

See also **Acronymaniacs** and **Lizjoneses**.

Endorsees

Classic Status

Here's a really nice post from Janice about me.

In Other Words...

Look! Someone says they think I'm great. I'm pointing this out because I need more of you to do the same.

Comment

Endorsees are desperately clunky self-promoters whose M.O. is, with touched faux humility, to share a complimentary status update that *someone else* has posted about them. This *should* be funny, because it's so insane – but it's actually more than a little bit tragic. It's like going up to someone you find attractive, tapping them on the shoulder and saying, "take a look at this note I've kept hold of from a girl/boy when I was thirteen, saying they want to go out with me - it proves I have a track record of being liked, so, really, you'd be missing out if you didn't fall in love with me too...now would be fine".

See also **Breakdowns** and **Clangers**.

Facebloggers

Classic Status

(Very, very long and tedious blog entry).

In Other Words...

My dullness gives all Facebookers a bad name, but I'm *too* dull to realise it.

Comment

Status updates on Facebook were once limited to 160 characters - now you can stick up to 60,000 on there before the Men In Blue start smashing your back door in. It's an invitation to be self-indulgent that the Faceblogger is powerless to resist. To the rest of us, Faceblogging is like Pizza Hut Salad Bar Cheating (PHSBC). For the uninitiated, PHSBC is a salad bar maximisation technique, where you fill your buffet bowl with small, dense salad materials such as sweet corn, then top it with a flat, wider lid of cucumber slices, on top of which you can build a tower of food, dense and compressed at the bottom, lighter on top, all resulting in what's known as a Leaning Tower of Pizza Hut. Like Faceblogging, most of us know PHSBC is possible, and occasionally we will take a small liberty - but routinely exploiting the loophole to the nth degree is completely inappropriate.

See also **News Readers** and **Shit Sharers**.

Fakedowns

Classic Status

 That's it - I don't think I can do this anymore...

In Other Words...

 I CAN do this any more, but admitting that wouldn't get me any attention.

Comment

 Fakedowns are attention-seekers who throw out super dramatic status updates as casually as they'd have a cup of tea, crying wolf for all the people who genuinely *are* at the end of their tether. You can *usually* tell who the latter are – for starters they are probably not writing about it on Facebook – but of course you can't know that for sure, and that's what makes the Fakedown so annoying. They deserve to be punished with the support and attention of a Shoulder - they won't get it though, because the two can sniff out one another's insincerity...you can't kid a kidder and all that. Instead, they will suck all the energy out of their poor, worried friends, who will have no choice but to take their cries for help seriously.

See also **Breakdowns**.

Foodfuckers

Classic Status

 Yummy: quinoa rarebit & double-dipped Elk burger at the House of Bone popup @ Selfridges.

In Other Words…

 I know a HELL of a lot about food.

Comment

 Foodfuckers are food porn bores. Posts from this Facebooker can vary according to their budget, social status and geographical location – from an 'arty' picture of a home-made fruit salad, to a gushing description of a 19 course gastronomic wank-fest in the test kitchen of a triple Michelin starred 'eating house' in the Pyrenees. Either way, it's a tyrannical show of culinary superiority by men with small penises.

See also **Bakers**, **Mwahnkers** and **Whoopsaboasties**.

Frustrartists

Classic Status

 (Yet another arty photo taken by the Frustrartist).

In Other Words...

 I am talented, but only showcase my talents on Facebook, because I won't risk artistic rejection.

Comment

 When someone publishes more than five Instagram photos in a week as status updates, they are trying to tell the world something: that they have a serious, unappreciated talent. Some people even post poems on Facebook. POEMS?! It's like writing your CV on a toilet wall – it's quite clear that nothing good can come of it. But that's the point. Not only is the Frustrartist *aware* of the futility of showcasing their talents on a site where the most creative thing that people want to see is a video of a cat wearing sunglasses – that's *why* they do it. The Frustrartist uses Facebook to enhance the sense that they have talent that is being denied, without any opportunities arising that would force their hand, and make them actually do something about it.

See also **Foodfuckers** and **Runners and Riders**.

Gamblegags

Classic Status

 (Insert sick joke here).

In Other Words...

 I see myself as the go-to guy for sick jokes, even though telling them on social media is massively risky.

Comment

 Every social circle (and What's App group) contains a proud peddler of inappropriate jokes - jokes about dead celebrities, jokes about paedophiles, jokes about anything just plain wrong (three ticks for Jimmy Saville, still). Joke peddlers like to smash out round after round of jokes in bad taste: but as JK Rowling will tell you, these days you can't even safely express ill-thought-through opinions without causing massive offence, let alone go around telling jokes that actually SET OUT to upset people. Look after the tragic Gamblegag in your life then. No-one's laughing. The lawyers are watching. They're still treating Facebook as their Locker Room. So every gag is a gamble.

See also **Comediens and Twatfaces**.

Ghosties

Classic Status

 (Nothing...ever).

In Other Words...

 There is no-one here: only tumbleweed and the dusty remains of a short-lived Facebook existence.

Comment

 Ghosties are people who set up a Facebook account several years ago; they immediately made contact with their main friends, but then, within days, promptly gave up on the whole sorry business so they could spend their time doing something more worthwhile. And they've never been back. However, unbeknownst to them, their Facebook persona lingers on, leading a kind of ghost existence. They are tagged in photos from old parties. Their haircut might be discussed. They are invited to new parties. They are mentioned in posts and threads. But they will never reply, because they are not there. I love these people – they are kings. You get a kind of Super 8, silent movie impression of their lives – it is romantic and old fashioned and full of pathos, and in my *dreams*, I'd be just like them. I'm not though.

See also **Ghoulies** and **Peeping Toms**.

Ghoulies

Classic Status

 (Nothing...ever).

In Other Words...

 I desperately want you to think I'm not bothered about Facebook because I am secretly a depraved addict.

Comment

 The Ghoulie's behaviour *appears* much the same as that of the Ghostie – they are, apparently, not there. But whilst Ghosties are simply off enjoying the fresh air, Ghoulies *are* there really. And it's about more than being a Peeping Tom. It's a *stance*, a declaration of superiority: they desperately want to be *seen* to be not there. So how do you spot the difference? Tease them. If they are Ghosties, they will not respond. But the shocking truth about Ghoulies is that they are *secretly indulging* in Facebook, like a repressed Victorian Dad who denounces 'sins of the flesh', but actually spends all his spare time masturbating furiously in fishnets. Facebook's forbidden fruits are the Ghoulie's guilty pleasure - they cannot get by without their secret daily fix of other peoples' cat news etc. So when you tease them they'll *respond* all right: by hunting you down...

See also **Ghosties**.

Groupers

Classic Status

 (An invitation to join their group or like their page).

In Other Words...

 I've invited you because you'll be too lazy or clueless to refuse.

Comment

 Groupers ruthlessly sign up you, their 'friends', as members of a Facebook group, knowing that you will almost certainly ask no questions. It's much like being leafleted by a loved one. Groupers also invite you to 'like' their professional pages - and it seemingly doesn't matter AT ALL what those pages are for, or how appropriate a liker you are. But if *you* ran, say, a sanitary products importation company, why would you want a scruffy 30 something male to be a public advocate for your product range? In the unlikely event that a tampon fan is one day scouring Facebook for sanitary product importation companies, and stumbles across yours, their initial sense of admiration at seeing that it has 72 likes will surely soon be tempered by feelings of dismay, when they realise that you've railroaded children, old people and scruffy 30 something males into unwittingly becoming 'the face of foreign tampons'?

See also **Conspirabores** and **Groupees**.

Groupees

Classic Status

 'Insert Facebooker's name here' has just liked the page 'San-im-port UK'.

In Other Words...

 Suggest ANYTHING, and I'll back you.

Comment

 These are the Facebookers who are actively *delighted* to be subjugated by Groupers - in fact deriving a great deal of self-worth from being invited to join this group, that group and the other group. They are not bothered how appropriate the request - they will basically join *anything*, and are therefore socially irresponsible, and would have fitted in rather *too* well in Nazi Germany.

See also **Groupers** and **Pro Likers**.

Handsomes

Classic Status

'Insert Facebooker's Name Here' has changed his/her cover photo. (And so has their partner).

In Other Words...

Hey guys, here's another pic showing how great me and my girlfriend/boyfriend/spouse look together.

Comment

It's not about what the Handsome *says*, it's about what *we see*. Like Coverers, all they ever seem to do is change their cover photo – but the Handsome only changes it from one smoochy woochy photo (demonstrating what a handsome couple they and their partner/girlfriend/boyfriend/spouse are) to another. Every week they get more thrillingly hunky and sexy. Oh, and the partner will also change their photo at the same time, natch. This is use of Facebook as a form of mutual validation: "Check me out, I'm with someone photogenic. And so is she! Our genes are good. Imagine if we had kids - they'd be models or something...how cool is that?". Well done!

See also **Coverers**.

Hey-ho-huffles

Classic Status

 Hey-ho. (And then on for about three pages).

In Other Words...

 I am calm and benign - I'm just saying that 900 bad things happened to me today, and now I need a white wine.

Comment

 Hey-ho-huffles are super-nice, squeaky clean types who've had a bad day. They tend to be contented stay-at-home earth mothers, middle class charity workers or funky seniors – and since, unlike the rest of us when we've had a bad day, they don't snap at someone on their commute, pick a fight with their partner, or scream at their kids, they turn instead to Facebook. These aren't explosive *Falling Down* style rants - rather an extensive detailing of how, for example, they ended up making four trips to Mothercare due to various nappy disasters, were treated with utter disdain over several phone calls with Virgin Media Customer Services, and then dropped their door key down a drain. Whilst it would drive most people to murder, the sum total of the Hey-ho-huffle's struggle usually manifests itself as little more than the need to have a larger-than-usual glass of white wine at 7:30pm.

See also **Facebloggers**, **Pissed Parents** and **Woemers**.

Horn Bombers

Classic Status

 Fancy some dumplings '@Insert Facebooker's Partner's Name Here'?

In Other Words...

 We have actual sex! And we are going to do it now. Just imagine that...

Comment

 This Facebooker's crime is to drop public 'horn bomb' hints to their partner that they wish to 'action' some sexual congress RIGHT NOW. (See also Poo Posters for news on other Facebookers who can't get over how amazing it is that they can have sex). But of course, posting ANY kind of coded message on Facebook is like pinning up an envelope with 'PRIVATE MESSAGE WRITTEN WITHIN, DO NOT OPEN' written on it in massive capital letters. Or 'LOOK AT ME'. These utterly transparent horn bombs are rankly distasteful to the observer: the written equivalent of that heavily tongue-based kissing that only your newly divorced mum does with her new boyfriend, because she wants your eyes to bleed. It's as erotic as someone coming clomping expansively out of the loo at work and wafting a copy of The Sun in your face, before exclaiming 'Aaaagh, that's better, but I'd leave it 10 minutes,' and dropping the violated tabloid on your desk.

See also **Poo Posters** and **TMI's.**

Indians

Classic Status

 (Photo) The view from my veranda this morning in Varanasi…

In Other Words…

 You're going to be well-jel because I'm stickin' it to the man, TRAVELLING. In INDIA! I'm soooo random!!

Comment

 These aren't people who are Indian. That would be ridiculous. Instead, these are people who use Facebook to demonstrate how much more fun they are having than you, because they are 'travelling'. Usually in India. The really great thing about 'travelling', the Indian is saying, is that it means they are not at work - whilst you *are*. That's a) why they are on Facebook showing off about it rather than actually off doing things and b) why they regularly specify that they have "only 6 weeks to go" or "are on Day 52" or whatever. I.E. 'You're at work, ha ha – I've been off work for 52 whole days!!!'. Frankly though, if 'travelling' is primarily appealing because it's better than working, it's got to do better, and I like to read these posts from the comfort of my desk each morning, imagining the Indian's tummy-ache as I enjoy an over-priced latte and plan my TV viewing for the evening.

See also **Frustrartists** and **Whoopsaboasties**.

Lizjoneses

Classic Status

 I can't believe people are slagging off Margaret Thatcher. Without her there would be no (etc etc)...

In Other Words...

 I am a smug dick.

Comment

 Named after fascist sociopath and Daily Fail 'writer' Liz Jones. And in honour of the Daily Fail in general. The Daily Mail is basically The Sun for people who think they are clever. Most Sun readers are sated by the sight of beasts, whereas breasts just make Daily Mail readers angry, like everything else. And in my book, anger is a greater threat to mankind than the rather bewildering worship of breasts, as long as that worship is pathetic but private.

See also **Emoticonservatives**.

Location Location Locationaters

Classic Status

'Insert Facebooker's Name Here' is in Café Rouge, Staines.

In Other Words...

I'm telling you exactly where I am because I have unresolved long-term guilt issues.

Comment

To an LLL, it ain't where you're from, it's where you're *at*. Even if where you're *at* is just Morrisons in Stoke. Over time, they have developed a deep-seated compulsion to provide us with an up-to-the-minute, satellite-accurate picture of where they are, and I believe that it's driven by a form of *guilt*. At some point in the past they have probably either been:

a) caught with their underpants down OR
b) an accessory to a failed attempt at a minor crime EG robbing a post office with a water pistol.

Now, in a strange form of self electronic tagging, they attempt to assuage the tap, tap, tap of these guilty feelings by 'reporting in' regularly to the rest of the world – not with any news as such, just with a damned near *crucial* update on where they are currently sitting.

See also **Tag Slags**.

Messengers

Classic Status

 I want to see how many of you will take time to share this fab poem about happiness written by a 9 year-old...

In Other Words...

 I buy into all the daftest wishful thinking bollocks you can think of – hey, why don't you join me??!!

Comment

 Messengers tend to be 'blessed' devotees of Rhonda Byrne's spazfest *The Secret*, and other similarly infuriating real-life avoidance techniques such as Mindfulness. They are prone to pasting long, supposedly life-affirming round robin stories, photos and poems, and encouraging people to 'share' what they have posted. Sometimes with a vague implied threat that if you don't, really bad shit will happen to you. Pleasingly, no-one ever *does* share them.

See also **Conspirabores** and **Quoters**.

Mwahnkers

Classic Status

 Bubbly in the Soho Hotel with the girls from #RHOCheshire xx mwah xx #cokedup #mybad #mwah

In Other Words...

 Shoot me, now, for my own good and yours.

Comment

 Mwahnkers are media wankers who work in a creative industry but have allowed themselves to become suit-wearing corporate zombies. They appear on Facebook only to sully it with their awful Mwahnker outlook and way of talking. They air-kiss - mwah - a lot. They actually *write* mwah. They fill Facebook with meaningless phrases like 'my bad'. They quote their favourite TV shows and talk about how AMAZING *Succession* is, all the time. Other than that they only ever a) mention that they are drinking champagne or b) tag the hotel they are staying in, but only when it is Babington House, never when it's the Travelodge in Salford or c) promote whatever shite their company is working on, without any sense of irony, because they are not making any money themselves, and if you worked for McVities, you wouldn't stick up pictures of biscuits all the time would you?

See also **Bakers**.

News Readers

Classic Status

 Kelvin has won Strictly!!

In Other Words...

 I'm 68 and I'm excited - because I'm ON A COMPUTER!!!

Comment

 News Readers (also known as *Old Age Mentioners*) are the people who attempt to reveal major headline stories to us as if they are literally the only person in the world who has access to electricity, information or a television. They are the social media embodiment of your dad pointing out things that quite clearly do not need pointing out, such as "It's raining" or "Del Boy fell through the bar". News Readers are usually over 65 – Anna Ford, you'd bloody *love* Facebook – and their Facebook behaviour reflects a doomed ongoing effort to try and be modern. They think that because they are sitting on their laptop – or let's be honest, possibly their circa 2008 era Dell desktop – when they discover something that's happened in the world, that means they are discovering something *before* the rest of the world, because the rest of the world waits for the Ten O'Clock News. To be fair though, the rest of *their* world does.

See also **Facebloggers** and **Shit Sharers**.

Nonversationalists

Classic Status

Any thoughts on the perfect menu for an American Indian vegan?

In Other Words...

I already have the answer to my question, but I need one of you to tee me up so I can show off with it.

Comment

Nonversationalists instigate non-conversations on Facebook – one-way written dialogues designed to encourage just enough input from other people to create the *impression* that a conversation is taking place, but no more. The classic manoeuvre is to make a statement, prompting a fairly predictable quick-fire comment from someone else, which then allows them to go on and complete everything that needs to be said on the subject via a long and exceptionally carefully-worded monologue. Nonversationalists have *plenty* to say, and they know exactly how best to say it, so as far as they are concerned, conversations would be a lot better if they had full control of them and played all the key parts – whereas once they start involving others in 'their' conversation, it runs the very real risk of failing to live up to their very precise expectations.

See also **Speed Freaks**.

Pendings

Classic Status

 (Nothing – they are waiting for you to risk welcoming them into your life by accepting their friend request).

In Other Words...

 Hurry up! I'm waiting. You can't ignore me forever.

Comment

 Most established Facebookers have a small column of people hidden away near the top their screen: they're the elephants in your Facebook room, the dirty secrets you thought you never had, the mysteries you have a feeling you don't want to delve into. I am talking of course about the people who have sent you a friend request, but you have no idea who they are. Or maybe you vaguely remember meeting them at a party and having absolutely nothing in common. Or perhaps you know *exactly* who they are, but at no point in the last 20 years did you ever think about them - and now that they've ACTIVELY HUNTED YOU DOWN, you're a bit scared. No matter – all these people are your Pendings. Theoretically, the Pending is none the wiser that all this is going on in your head – the silence that has met their friend request is better than the brutal truth. It is better, after all, to be ignored at the bar, than told you are too much of a w**ker to serve.

See also **Ghosties** and **Ghoulies**.

Pissed Parents

Classic Status

 Oh, I just LOVE doing the washing up at midnight.

In Other Words…

 I am married, I am tired, I am drunk, I am cross.

Comment

 Pissed Parents usually materialise when their partner has gone out to have a good time without them, leaving them to ineptly look after some children or domestic duties *alone*. They're angry because they'd rather be drinking prosecco at a leisurely pace and dicking around on their laptop/phone, safe in the knowledge that their partner is at other end of the sofa doing the same thing, and is thus a) only having the same amount of fun as them and b) available to share/take on the burden of the work. Instead, after a stressful and extended evening of struggling to get the kids to bed, it's then too late to eat, and then the kitchen needs tidying etc. An attempt to tame their sky-rocketing blood pressure with the rapid ingestion of alcohol follows, but those residual tensions have not been properly processed, and the moment that big blue Facebook banner meets their eyes…boom…

See also **Hey-ho-huffles** and **Sideswipes**.

Poo Posters

Classic Status

 Look at my baby's amazing poo.

In Other Words...

 I don't get out much - when I do, stay away from me, because I will corner you aggressively with my baby photos.

Comment

 Similar but, despite the name, not the same as, Shit Sharers. Poo Posters are those parents so deluded about the interestingness of their children that they think we don't mind their posts about poo. And in one instance, I really do mean that someone I know posted a picture of their child's poo. These are people who, and this is essentially all it boils down to, have managed to have *sex*, and then some time afterwards, a baby has come out of their tummy - but it turns out that *them* having a baby is a whole different thing to every *other* person in the world having a baby. Basically, you know that feeling you have until you are about 12, that you, genuinely, are a little bit more special and important, and experience life far more acutely than everyone else? Well I suspect that for these people, that feeling never really went away. Oh, and for the record, the dads are the worst...

See also **Shit Sharers** and **TMI's**.

Pro Likers

Classic Status

 (Nothing – too busy 'liking' everything other people say).

In Other Words...

 I haven't really thought through what 'liking' your post about your dad dying will look like.

Comment

 These indiscriminate scattergun 'likers' of *everything* undermine the relative quality of your very best and most lovingly-crafted updates. Worse, they use this one response whether you're telling them a joke or telling them your Dad's just died. There ARE more options you know - they've been around for a while, so USE them.

See also **Groupees and Tag Slags**.

Quoters

Classic Status

 "If you haven't found it yet, keep looking". Steve Jobs.

In Other Words...

 I will never use my own words to sum up how I feel.

Comment

 This is the Facebooker who only ever communicates or tells us how they are feeling via a quote. During the main 'deification of the late capitalist Steve Jobs' period in 2011, he was the main man to quote from – and some people are still unable to shake this peculiar habit. Others though will quote freely from *anyone*, as long as what they've said sounds meaningful or mysterious. Greta, Daddy Pig, Tommy (or Timmy) Mallett: all, it seems, equally acceptable. Quoters are essentially saying that *nobody* can sum up how they feel better than someone they will never meet, and possibly had never heard of until they found a quote they liked the look of. Sometimes I even suspect the tail wags the dog, and how they feel is actually *determined* by a quote they've stumbled across. As a kind, they are never happier than when in a 'quote off' with another of their ilk.

See also **Messengers**.

Runners and Riders

Classic Status

 11.5k hill session tonight – feeling good. Up at 6 tomorrow for 40k ride B4 work then Peloton!

In Other Words...

 I can run, and I have a very light bike. You may not think that's a big deal, but let me fill you in on the details.

Comment

 You just went for a run? Great. Can you please tell us how many 'K' it was and what your time was? Ooh, and also, how that time compares to your usual? Oh, you've got the cool new *Jogtwatz* 'app' that uploads that info automatically to Facebook as well? Brilliant! What's that?! You've got a ridiculously expensive road bike too, and you just did – how many?!?! 84 hardcore K? And how does *that* compare to your usual? Gosh, you *are* fit etc etc...

See also **Bakers, Frustrartists** and **Mwahnkers**.

Sagatarians

Classic Status

My roof troubles continue: woken by a knock on the door this morning, my neighbour telling me that...(etc etc)...

In Other Words...

Yes, I really am on about THAT again.

Comment

No, Sagatarians are not people who only eat the elderly. And nor are they Sagitarians - although statistically, some of them must be. No - Sagatarians are people who love a saga. It all begins with a *problem* - usually something unexciting like a leaky roof or a detached retina (boring...so 2015 before the world fell apart). It won't be a serious issue – but the first time they mention it on Facebook, they get one or two sympathetic comments and a bit of positive attention, and the damage, unfortunately, is done. The problem doesn't get solved, and bingo: the happy Sagatarian has got themselves a saga. They will nurture and feed off it, and it's a two-way cancerous relationship: it becomes their lifeblood and vice versa. And on Facebook, they have a captive audience who WILL be updated with every latest instalment, whether they like it or not. (They don't).

See also **Breakdowns, Fakedowns, Hey-Ho-Huffles** and **Woe-mers**.

Shit Sharers

Classic Status

 Just watching Corrie.

In Other Words...

 I really am just watching Corrie.

Comment

 A serious problem on Facebook is the oversharer, or Shitsharer: they risk spoiling it for the rest of us by giving our world a bad name. If you have an aunt who has read about Facebook in The Daily Mail or discussed it with their golf club cronies - you know, the way they might discuss 'immigration', looking like they are chewing a wasp, without ever feeling the need to be well-informed - their impression of Facebook is of a world where people write what they ate for breakfast. The trouble is, there ARE people who write what they ate for breakfast. *And* what they ate for lunch. *And* the snacks that they had in between etc. They, are Shit Sharers. Once again, to be fair, Facebook is just providing a valuable service in reducing such people to the very essence of their personality – boringness.

See also **Facebloggers** and **TMI's**.

Shoulders

Classic Status

(Nothing – they are watching and waiting for vulnerable people they can offer support to).

In Other Words...

I'm slightly creepy.

Comment

Shoulders (also known as *Smarm*-maritans) are sweaty 'mature student' type single men in their forties or fifties who hover on Facebook late at night, ready to offer a shoulder to cry on, way too quickly, to any female Facebook friends with a crisis. At the first sign of upset, they will pop up immediately with a sympathetic comment, offering solace, support, and maybe a 'word to the wise,' usually backed up with smileys and emoticons to reinforce the fact that they definitely aren't just sniffing out the possibility of sex with an extremely vulnerable woman. They are the Speed Freaks of the empathy world. If there's a *bloke* with a problem though, fuck it – he can do one. Only the ladies get The Shoulder's attention.

See also **Pro Likers** and **Speed Freaks**.

Sideswipes

Classic Status

 Well, you know who your friends are…

In Other Words…

 Someone has done something bad to me. Just letting you know, so you can ask me about it.

Comment

 Nope, it's not that kind of swiping to the side. The Sideswipe's M.O. is to post a short, vaguely cryptic but clearly damning statement about a mystery third party - an ex partner, a work colleague, or most commonly, a friend who is now no longer a friend, although they are as yet unaware of it. That's problematic though. Because if that person wasn't really someone you remotely liked in the first place, they wouldn't be a Facebook friend, in which case, they wouldn't see your message; whilst if they *were* a friend of any kind, they could well be on Facebook, but if you hate them, you'll have de-friended them, so again, they won't see the message. So exactly who then, is the sideswipe for? *Us* of course. If we don't ask about it, that's fine, it'll at least be assumed that we're worrying about them. And if we do ask, that's also good – we'll get a direct message heaping shit onto the absent third party, or we'll be ignored, to up the intrigue.

See also **Fakedowns**.

Smuggers

Classic Status

 A picture of me with my girls. (Taken at end of an Ultra Marathon, wearing a 'Save Orphaned Whales' t-shirt).

In Other Words...

 Hey, check out how modest I am. Oh OK, I admit it, I'm a totally epic hero.

Comment

 Whilst Chuggers assault you on the street for cash, Smuggers batter you on Facebook with their own *personal* charity heroics, employing the Facebook faux modesty trick of making it look almost accidental that they've just revealed how totally skill-balls and Major Tom-esque they are. They've been on a bike ride to help kids with cancer. They've worn a hair shirt for 40 days and 40 nights to help fund a prosthetic leg for a cute local guide dog with a speech defect. They've signed a petition to STOP THE WAR. All of these things make them look caring, ace and sexy, especially when they are revealed by accident. And then, as *well* as feeling irritated by how much more of a good person they are than you, you're compelled to head to their Just Giving page and make a donation.

See also **Bakers and Whoopsaboasties**.

Snarketeers

Classic Status

Oca*don't* Zoom.

In Other Words...

I am delighting in the immense power that social networking has given *me*, the unhappy customer.

Comment

Snarketeers use the Good Book as a reverse-marketing tool for companies that have not delivered (sometimes literally), dishing out instant customer service justice for everyone else's future benefit. Most companies could only ever dream of *positive* online endorsements as transparently authentic and powerful as this. Posts such as these should fill us all with delight at the thought of some blood sucking marketing executive trawling through Facebook for brand mentions, and the rising of their blood pressure as they start to realise their company's contempt for its customer base is finally catching up with them. (Author's note: Ocado Zoom used for illustrative purposes only. Nothing wrong with them probably, wouldn't know, prefer walking to Lidl).

See also **Brazen Mavens**.

Social Knitworkers

Classic Status

@CarolJane meet @SineadByrne. S, C's just moved nr u & needs a builder (& wine drinking buddy LOL!!). Enjoy!

In Other Words...

Without me, all of *you*, my *friends*, would be f**ed and connection-less.

Comment

Everyone's got a 'superfriend' – you know, the loud one that sloshes white wine around like it's rainwater and holds together all your social lives. Being an 'introducer' like this is not without its rewards: seeing your disparate friends uniting through the one thing they have in common – you – can be a great feeling. But it's also a gamble not for the faint-hearted, because seeing your disparate friends discover that they absolutely hate each other can leave them blaming the one thing they have in common: you. But being a friendship maven on Facebook is different: it carries no risks. The first time they meet, Carol may conclude that Sinead is a waspish bitch she never wants to see again, but the Social Knitworker knows that no-one will ever find that out, whilst his/her social importance will still be there for all to see. So a virtual introducer is 50% more of a glory hunter than someone doing it offline.

See also **Brazen Mavens** and **Clangers**.

Spamateurs

Classic Status

I am totally living the dream and you could be too - it is your time to shine. This is not a scam!!

In Other Words...

I have paid money to believe all of the above – if I tell you all about it too, maybe it'll somehow turn out ok.

Comment

Spamateurs are inadvertent, amateur spammers who have unwittingly signed themselves up to facilitate some kind of internet marketing (spam) campaign. This is how it works. The Spamateur reaches a point in their life where a change is needed – namely, more money for less grief. The promise of easy cash through internet marketing (spam) proves irresistible. What they don't realise is that internet marketing (spam) actually means spam (also known as internet marketing). They leap in, in good faith. They attend 'webinars' (web seminars labeled as webinars by people who were bullied at school) organised by 'inspirational web marketing gurus' (who were bullied at school) who naturally have their best interests at heart. And then they tell *you* ALL about it. And bombard you with horrendously badly written links for blogging tools and internet marketing programmes.

See also **Conspirabores** and **Messengers**.

Speed Freaks

Classic Status

 (Nothing – they're too busy scrabbling to be the first to comment on yours).

In Other Words...

 I am competitive, especially when it comes to being the first to comment on your posts: it's kind of my 'thing'.

Comment

 Speed Freaks are always hovering, determined to be the first person to comment on all other people's posts. The true Speed Freak is 'on call' 24/7, waiting, poised by their computer or 'communications device'. A good day is one where their record is untarnished – first to the punch on all occasions. They don't have time to chat though – once they have achieved their objective of winning the all-important race to be the first to comment on something, they're off, on to the next project, waiting to spread a bit more of their speed-of-response based magic. If you want to upset a Speed Freak or keep him/her quiet, simply beat them to it. You'll be met with an infuriated silence - because commenting second is for losers.

See also **Pro Likers**.

Tag Slags

Classic Status

(A constant and never-ending frenzy of tagging).

In Other Words...

I don't *like* tagging - I *love* it.

Comment

Tag Slags play fast and loose with their photo tagging. They'll tag anything and anyone in the name of getting stuff properly labeled. They're mothercrushin' crazy about tagging. I suspect that what they *really* want is to be a shopkeeper with one of those cool pricing guns, so they can tag stuff willy-nilly. It's as if they are logging all the exhibits in a free-to-view online museum – and historically, it may well prove that they are providing an invaluable service. But the question still remains: why do they do it? It could be that they're seeking to anchor themselves at the centre of things, with a reinvention of the past that writes them indelibly into it. Either that or the thing I said about the cool pricing guns.

See also **Dredgers** and **Pro Likers**.

Technobabblers

Classic Status

 Infected with delta search toolbar, ran a malware tool, found a backdoor Trojan.

In Other Words...

 You may think I'm a dweeb, but I'm *actually* a geek, which means that soon I'll be so rich I could buy you.

Comment

 The Technobabbler will usually just post a link to an anti-virus cheat, or an article lambasting the latest Mac OSX. If they *do* ever a post a status update or comment on anything, a word like 'linux' will slip in there and the rest of the world will just scratch their heads and shrug dismissively - which is silly, because it has been categorically proven that the geek shall inherit the earth. Conclusion: go and find out who or what 'linux' is.

See also **Brazen Mavens**.

TMI's

Classic Status

 Really bad diarrhoea and vomiting today.

In Other Words...

 I can disassociate myself entirely from my frank medical admissions and the effect they may have on others.

Comment

 Givers of too much information are a spin-off from Shit Sharers, but definitely should not be confused, confusingly, with Poo Posters. Their USP isn't a running stream of conscious commentary of every aspect of their daily lives – instead, it's *fewer* posts, always containing more graphic, stomach-churning personal information than you would ever want to know. It's not done with any desire to shock – it's just that they tend to be very, er, 'medical', about things. Which isn't always what you want shoved in your face when you're checking out your Facebook over breakfast thanks.

See also **Poo Posters** and **Shit Sharers**.

Twatfaces

Classic Status

 (Via Twitter) Simon, why the surprised look? Oh...

In Other Words...

 This kind of live commentary belongs on Twitter not Facebook, but I think I'm funny enough to get away with it.

Comment

 What's right for a tweet - a quick-fire, impersonal gag whilst watching X-Factor, or a stream of consciousness bore-statement about your football team's injury crisis - is *rarely* right for a status update on Facebook. It's the equivalent of handing your CV round at a family party: it's inappropriate, and makes you look like a bit of a dick. Actively diverting your tweets to Facebook however, as Twatfaces do, is unforgivable. By virtue of being on Twitter, the Twatface is a relatively established social networker, who understands the way these things work – which makes them worryingly deluded.

See also **Comediens and Twitfaces**.

Twitfaces

Classic Status

 Simon, why the surprised look? Oh...

In Other Words...

 I am new to Facebook, but will soon discover that I'd be better off on Twitter.

Comment

 Twitfaces are novice Facebookers in a transitional stage. Although they may well share similar status updates with Twatfaces, they are completely different. After resisting computers, mobile phones and then social networking, these late adopters have dipped a toe into Facebook, but haven't yet learned what it's for. But they will – when they discover their talent for pithy witticisms goes un-appreciated on a forum more useful for people with news about dogs or babies. Twitter, to them, sounds like something for terrible wankers. Give it six months though, and they'll be one of them.

See also **News Readers** and **Twitfaces**.

Whoopsaboasties

Classic Status

(Photo) Check out this friendly squirrel in my garden...

In Other Words...

Check out my fucking massive garden: I've got a bigger garden than you, your garden is shit, mine is incredible.

Comment

Whoopsaboasties are Facebookers who indulge in stealth boasting - posting apparently innocuous photos, stories or comments which *actually* reveal them to be FUCKING AMAZING. Photos are particularly effective for a Whoopsaboastie, because you can *label* them as being one thing – EG "Me and the cat watching television" – whilst allowing the photographic evidence, just coincidentally you understand, to reveal just how special you are. IE "Here's me and the cat watching my epic 64 inch plasma, yes I've got my shirt off, yes I've got a six pack".

See also **Bakers, Brazen Mavens** and **Smuggers**.

Woemers

Classic Status

F***ing Virgin Media. I'm sat here with my broken leg, I've just spent TWO hours on the phone (etc etc)...

In Other Words...

I'm going to patiently set about making you realise that my life is AWFUL.

Comment

It's easy being a moany pessimistic bastard in real life: negativity can just pour out, gathering an unstoppable momentum, and before you know it, everyone around you is thoroughly depressed. Job done. But try communicating the idea that life is *bad news* within the confines of a status update. It's not easy. Now try doing it again and again – in fact, never EVER write another positive status update. Being a Woemer is a *vocation*: it takes a conscious, committed effort, and the *best* are highly skilled practitioners. Woemable material can range from employment issues to gadget gripes to the grim details of a in-grown toenail. Variety is the key, and budding Woemers should beware: proper, *effective* woeming means you can never linger on a topic. Life is *shit*, you are *not* a nutter: but sustained and repeated woeming about one particular issue will turn you into one (see Sagatarians).

See also **Hey-Ho-Huffles** and **Sagatarians**.

Acknowledgements

Thanks to Will Moran for his endlessly patient and extremely poorly paid ghost writing.

Thanks to Delme for design skillz.

Thanks to A and B for being themselves.

And finally, thanks most of all to my Facebook friends, for keeping me entertained. Don't go changing.

What next?

If you enjoyed this book and want more Sauce Materials books then please:

Review us on Amazon, Good Reads and Waterstones

Follow us at instagram.com/sauce_materials

Like us at facebook.com/saucematerials

Join the Sauce Materials VIP Club for offers and giveaways at www.saucematerials.co.uk/vipclub

www.ingramcontent.com/pod-product-compliance
Lightning Source LLC
Chambersburg PA
CBHW070440010526
44118CB00014B/2120